Celebrations in My World

Sukkot

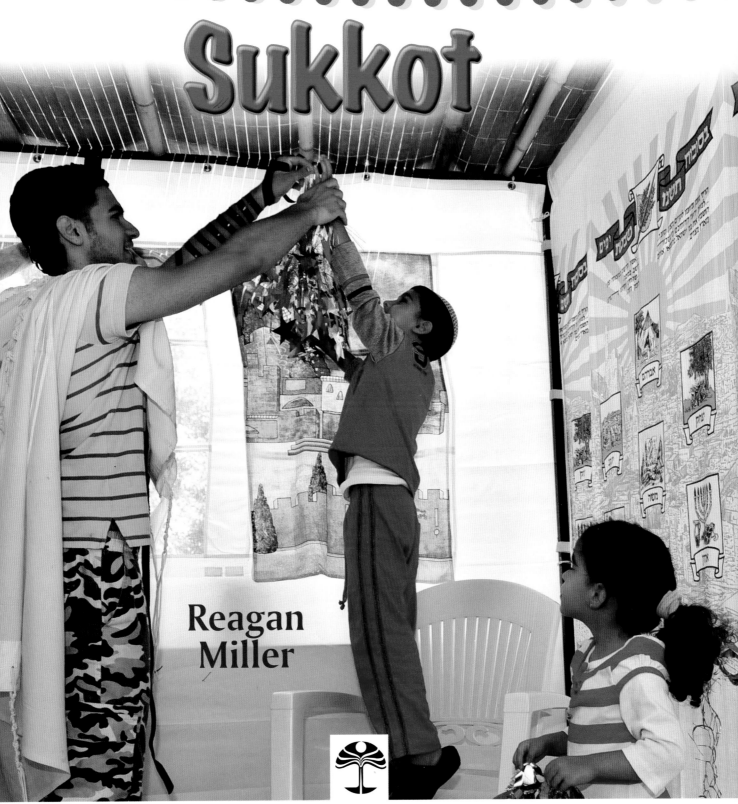

Reagan
Miller

Crabtree Publishing Company

www.crabtreebooks.com

Crabtree Publishing Company

www.crabtreebooks.com

Author: Reagan Miller
Coordinating editor: Chester Fisher
Series and project editor: Susan LaBella
Editor: Adrianna Morganelli
Proofreader: Molly Aloian
Editorial director: Kathy Middleton
Production coordinator: Katherine Berti
Prepress technician: Katherine Berti
Project manager: Kumar Kunal (Q2AMEDIA)
Art direction: Rahul Dhiman (Q2AMEDIA)
Cover design: Shruti Aggarwal (Q2AMEDIA)
Design: Cheena Yadav (Q2AMEDIA)
Photo research: Ekta Sharma (Q2AMEDIA)

Photographs:
AFP: Menahem Kahana: p. 16
Alamy: Israel images: p. 9, 20
AP Photo: Kevin Frayer: p. 11
BigStockPhoto: David Davis: p. 25
Corbis: Andy Aitchison: p. 13; Bettmann: p. 23
Dreamstime: Frenk and Danielle Kaufmann: p. 30; Rainer Schmittchen: p. 7
Fotolia: Sonya Etchison: p. 5; Graham Photography: p. 6; Noam: p. 18
Getty Images: Fred Mayer/Contributor: p. 15, 22; David Silverman/Staff: p. 12
Istockphoto: Noam Armonn: p. 19; Lisa Turay: p. 31
Photolibrary: North Wind Pictures: p. 10; Dan Porges: cover (background), p. 14, 27; Con Tanasiuk: p. 24
Photoshot: Chameleons Eye: p. 1
Reuters: Gil Cohen Magen: p. 26; Abed Omar Qusini: p. 17
Shutterstock: cover (foreground), folio image; MoonBloom: p. 21; Pjasha: p. 8
World Religions: Christine Osborne Pictures: p. 28, 29

Library and Archives Canada Cataloguing in Publication

Miller, Reagan
  Sukkot / Reagan Miller.

(Celebrations in my world)
Includes index.
ISBN 978-0-7787-4766-6 (bound).--ISBN 978-0-7787-4784-0 (pbk.)

  1. Sukkot--Juvenile literature. I. Title.
II. Series: Celebrations in my world

BM695.S8M54 2009   j296.4'33   C2009-905272-5

Library of Congress Cataloging-in-Publication Data

Miller, Reagan.
  Sukkot / Reagan Miller.
    p. cm. -- (Celebrations in my world)
  Includes index.
  ISBN 978-0-7787-4784-0 (pbk. : alk. paper) -- ISBN 978-0-7787-4766-6 (reinforced library binding : alk. paper)
  1. Sukkot--Juvenile literature. I. Title. II. Series.

BM695.S8M55 2010
296.4'33--dc22

                                    2009035005

Crabtree Publishing Company

www.crabtreebooks.com   1-800-387-7650

Printed in China/122009/CT20090915

Published in Canada
Crabtree Publishing
616 Welland Ave.
St. Catharines, ON
L2M 5V6

Published in the United States
Crabtree Publishing
350 Fifth Ave.
59th floor
New York, NY 10118

Published in the United Kingdom
Crabtree Publishing
Maritime House
Basin Road North, Hove
BN41 1WR

Published in Australia
Crabtree Publishing
386 Mt. Alexander Rd.
Ascot Vale (Melbourne)
VIC 3032

Contents

What is Sukkot?

Sukkot is one of three main holidays celebrated by people of the Jewish religion. Sukkot is celebrated in September or October. The dates of the holiday change from year to year but it always takes place during autumn.

Jewish people use a Jewish calendar. Sukkot is celebrated on the 15th day of the seventh month.

			September 2010 Elul 5766 - 8 Tishrei 5767			
				Wed	Thu	Fri	Sat
		1	2	3	4	5
		8 Elul	9 Elul Ki Tetze	10 Elul	11 Elul	12 Elul
6	7	8	9	10	11	12
13 Elul	14 Elul	15 Elul	16 Elul Ki Tavo	17 Elul	18 Elul	19 Elul
13	14	15	16	17	18	19
20 Elul	21 Elul	22 Elul	23 Elul S'lichot (evening) Nitzavim/Vayeledh	24 Elul	25 Elul	26 Elul
20	21	22	23	24	25	26
27 Elul	28 Elul	29 Elul Erev R.H.	Tishrei		Tishrei	4 Tishrei
27						
5 Tishrei						

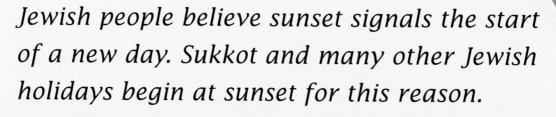

DID YOU KNOW?

Jewish people believe sunset signals the start of a new day. Sukkot and many other Jewish holidays begin at sunset for this reason.

Sukkot is celebrated for seven days and seven nights. It is one of the most cheerful Jewish holidays. It is a time when Jewish people remember their history, celebrate God's love, and are thankful for all they have.

Sukkot takes place in autumn, or fall. In many places, the leaves change color and fall from the trees.

What is Judaism?

The Jewish religion is called Judaism. Judaism is one of the oldest religions. It began nearly 4,000 years ago. Judaism is practiced by millions of people around the world. Judaism teaches that there is one God who is the creator of all things.

People who practice Judaism study the holy book called the Torah.

Judaism also teaches Jewish people to treat others with kindness and to help people in need. Helping others is an important part of celebrating Sukkot.

- A **synagogue** is a building where Jewish people go to pray.

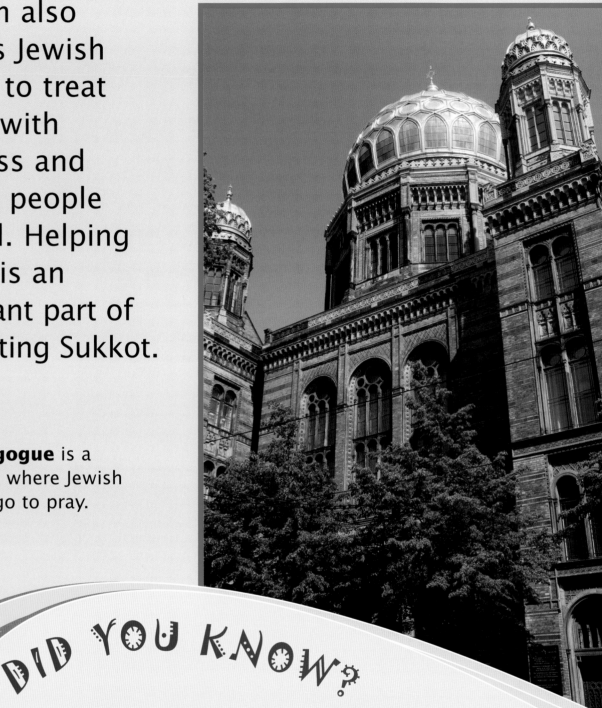

DID YOU KNOW?

The word Torah means "teachings" in the Hebrew language. The Torah teaches Jewish people how God wants them to live their lives.

7

The History of Sukkot

Sukkot celebrates Jewish history. Long ago, Jewish people lived as **slaves** in Egypt. God told Moses to lead the Jewish people out of Egypt and guide them to Israel. They spent 40 years walking through the desert before reaching Israel.

● The Jewish people walked through the Sinai desert to reach Israel.

Mediterranean Sea

Israel

Egypt

Sinai Desert

Red Sea

Middle East

This kind of booth is called a sukkah.

It was a difficult journey but God cared for the Jewish people. God made sure they had food, water, and shelter. During Sukkot, Jewish people remember how God cared for their **ancestors** during their journey to Israel.

DID YOU KNOW?

During their journey, God told the Jewish people to build booths for shelter. These booths were called sukkot. One booth is called a sukkah. The booths protected the Jewish people day and night.

9

Remembering the Harvest

During Sukkot, Jewish people also celebrate their ancestors' way of life. Many Jewish people became farmers once they reached Israel. The farmers **harvested** their **crops** in autumn. The crops had to be picked quickly so they did not spoil, or rot.

• Long ago, farmers did all of the work by hand. They did not have machines to help them like we do today.

During the harvest, a farmer would build a sukkah in his field. He slept in the sukkah so he could begin picking crops in the early morning without having to travel to the field from home. After the harvest, people praised God for providing them with the harvested food.

Children take part in a Sukkot pilgrimage, or trip, to thank God for the harvest.

DID YOU KNOW?

There are holidays to celebrate the autumn harvest in many places around the world. For example, in North America, many people celebrate a holiday called Thanksgiving.

11

Celebrate with a Sukkah

The sukkah is an important **symbol** of Sukkot. In the days leading up to Sukkot, many Jewish families are busy building their sukkah. Some build a sukkah in their backyards or on **balconies**.

In the Torah, God tells the Jewish people they must "dwell" in a sukkah for seven days.

DID YOU KNOW?

Sukkot is the Hebrew word for "booths." The holiday, Sukkot, is sometimes called the Festival of the Booths.

Other people work together to build a sukkah at their synagogue. During Sukkot, Jewish families eat, pray, and visit with friends and family in a sukkah. They are to think of their sukkah as home. Some people even sleep in a sukkah!

This boy is sleeping in his family's colorful sukkah.

13

Building a Sukkah

There are rules for building a sukkah. A sukkah must have at least two complete walls and the start of a third wall. The walls must be strong enough to stay standing when it is windy. A sukkah's roof must be made from plant parts that once grew from the ground, such as corn stalks or tree branches.

A sukkah can be small for just one person or large enough for hundreds of people.

A sukkah's roof is called the S'chach.

The roof must provide shelter to protect people from the sun. It must also have openings large enough for people to see the moon and stars at night.

DID YOU KNOW?

Sukkot is a time for people to feel close to nature. Spending time in a sukkah helps people connect with nature. Inside a sukkah, people can feel the sun, rain, and wind.

15

A Snazzy Sukkah!

Once the sukkah is built, it is time to decorate it! The sukkah is meant to be a cheerful place. Children often enjoy making decorations for the sukkah.

Children draw colorful pictures and banners or make mobiles to hang in their sukkah.

DID YOU KNOW?

Many people decorate their sukkah with fruits and vegetables from the autumn harvest. These decorations remind people to be thankful to God for helping the crops grow.

Children can show respect for Earth by making decorations using **recycled** materials. For example, children can use recycled paper to make paper chains to hang inside a sukkah. Children can decorate paper tissue rolls to make napkin rings to use during meals inside the sukkah.

Some people decorate using plastic fruits and vegetables so food is not wasted.

17

The Celebration Begins

The sukkah should be ready for the start of Sukkot. The celebration begins at sunset, and the first holiday meal starts soon after. Families eat meals together in their sukkah. On the first night of Sukkot, people welcome the celebration by saying a **blessing** and then lighting holiday candles.

A woman usually lights the Sukkot holiday candles.

18

A man says the Kiddush before the meal.

People say Kiddush, or a special holiday prayer, before the meal begins. They thank God for the blessing of the holiday and all that God has provided.

DID YOU KNOW?

The first two days of Sukkot are days of rest. People are not to do any work. The only work that is allowed is preparing meals.

A Scrumptious Sukkot!

Sukkot is a celebration of the autumn harvest. Many delicious meals prepared during this holiday are made from fresh fall fruits and vegetables.

This family is enjoying a delicious meal inside their sukkah.

Foods such as corn, pumpkins, pomegranates, apples, cranberries, and grapes are popular at this time of year. Soups and stews are often served during this holiday because they help keep people warm while eating outdoors in the sukkah.

People give thanks to God for a plentiful harvest.

DID YOU KNOW?

You can build a delicious sukkah! Use graham crackers and icing to make the walls. Use pretzels or cereal to make the roof. Decorate your sukkah with bits of fruit.

21

Sharing with Others

Sukkot is a time to be generous and to share. People invite family, friends, and neighbors to their sukkah to enjoy a meal together. People who are not Jewish are also welcome in the sukkah.

Family and friends share with one another at a Sukkot meal.

• The seven holy guests are known as the "Seven Shepherds of Israel." Moses is one of the holy guests.

In some communities, families plan "Sukkah Hops." Each family makes a treat for others to enjoy. Families then walk from sukkah to sukkah enjoying the treats and visiting with friends.

DID YOU KNOW?

On each night of Sukkot, Jewish people pray and invite a holy guest to their sukkah. The guests are Abraham, Moses, and other ancestors from the Torah.

23

Helping Others

During Sukkot, Jewish people give thanks to God for providing shelter and food. It is also a time to think about people who are in need. Some people collect food to give to food banks.

Sukkot is a time to give to others in need. This boy is giving food to people in need at a shelter.

Others help out at homeless shelters during the holiday. At some synagogues, people raise money to give to **charities** that work to help end hunger around the world.

● Some people make lists of the things they are thankful for. People can share these things with family and friends.

DID YOU KNOW?

Children can help people in need by collecting canned food to give to food banks. Children can also give their old clothing and toys to charities that can give them to children in need.

25

The Four Species

One of the most important symbols of Sukkot is called the four species. The four species are four different kinds of plants that grow in Israel. They include three types of branches and one kind of fruit.

Some people spend days looking for the most beautiful examples of each of the four species.

The four plants are myrtle, willow, palm shoot, and citron. During Sukkot, people use the four species for a special blessing. These four plants grow naturally in Israel.

Outside of Israel, they are shipped and sold in markets in the weeks before Sukkot.

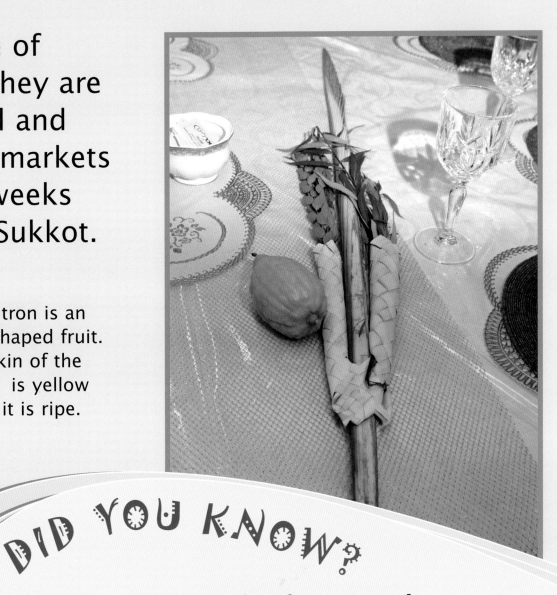

- The citron is an oval-shaped fruit. The skin of the citron is yellow when it is ripe.

DID YOU KNOW?

The myrtle, willow, and palm are tied together to form a lulav. *The citron, called an* etrog, *is kept separate from the* lulav.

27

Waves of Blessings

The four species are used in a special blessing every day during Sukkot except for on the **Sabbath**. The *lulav* is held in one hand and the *etrog* is held in the other.

A special blessing is said while waving the four species in all six directions—north, south, east, west, up, and down.

- A young boy holds the four plants as he says the special blessing.

This is done to celebrate the Jewish belief that God is everywhere. On the seventh day of Sukkot, people gather at a synagogue and perform a final blessing using the four species.

- The special blessing is done inside a sukkah or in a synagogue.

DID YOU KNOW?

Sukkot is celebrated before the rainy season begins in Israel. At the end of Sukkot, people pray to God for enough rain for plants to grow in the spring.

29

A Sukkot Snack

Sukkot is a wonderful time to enjoy the fruits, vegetables, and grains from the autumn harvest. Different kinds of foods are grown in different parts of the world.

Find out what kinds of foods are grown in your community. Let an adult help you use these foods to make a Sukkot snack, such as fruit salad.

● You can share your snack with family and friends.

Share your healthy treats with family and friends in your sukkah. Treats such as roasted pumpkin seeds and fruit salad are nutritious and delicious!

Harvest Fruit Salad: Choose fresh fruits grown in your area. Ask an adult to help you wash them and cut them into small pieces.

DID YOU KNOW?

Sukkot is a good time to visit a farm or orchard. You will learn which fruits and vegetables grow there. Sometimes, you can help pick your own fruits or vegetables to take home.

Glossary

ancestor One from whom a person or group of people is descended

balconies Platforms built at the side of buildings

blessing Asking for care and protection for something

charities Organizations that help people in need

crop A plant that can be grown and harvested

harvest The gathering of a crop; also the season when crops are gathered

recycled Things used more than once rather than being thrown away

Sabbath A Jewish holy day of rest and worship. It takes place each week from sunset on Friday to sunset on Saturday

slaves People who are owned by other people and forced to do hard work

symbol Something that stands for something else

synagogue A building where Jewish people worship

Index

Mr. Gator's up the Creek

By Julie McLaughlin

Illustrated by Ann Marie McKay

LEGACY PUBLICATIONS

For my family, friends, and all the children I have taught and loved.
Julie McLaughlin

For my grandchildren: Derrick, Robin, Mia, and Kimberly.
Ann Marie McKay

Text © 2005 Julie McLaughlin / Illustration © Ann Marie McKay
The illustrations were done in watercolor.

Library of Congress Control Number: 2004117313
ISBN 0-933101-23-6
Library of Congress Summary: A rejected alligator travels from his lake home
to a salt water creek, searching for acceptance.

Legacy Publications, 1301 Carolina Street, Greensboro, NC 27401 / www.pacecommunications.com
Printed in Canada by Friesens

The natural beauty

of wetlands in the South Carolina lowcountry

includes freshwater lakes, ponds, swamps, and coastal

salt marshes. These wetlands support a variety of plants

and provide food and shelter for abundant wildlife. We have had

the privilege of watching the wildlife in our own backyards,

and the fascinating wonders of nature never cease to amaze us.

Our hope is that MR. GATOR'S UP THE CREEK will not only

delight children, but also increase the awareness, appreciation,

and protection of our wetlands and their inhabitants.

Julie McLaughlin   Ann Marie McKay

Mr. Gator's tail moved back and forth like the rudder of a small boat as he began his early morning swim. Spring had finally arrived in the Carolina lowcountry, along with its glorious sights and smells.

The sweet fragrance of yellow jasmine and Cherokee roses
filled the air, and azaleas, bursting with color, bloomed
along the lake bank. Wood duck parents proudly presented
their new ducklings, while songbirds sang their familiar
tunes to welcome spring.

Bright rays of sunshine warmed his bumpy back
as Mr. Gator swam along admiring his lovely home.
Suddenly, he noticed a group of children walking
down the path by the lake.

"Why, I'll bet those children are looking for me,"
thought Mr. Gator, swimming closer to the shore. He swam
just near enough to overhear some of their conversation.

"Hey, Robin, which animal are you looking for?"
asked a freckle-faced boy.

"I want to see the new baby ducklings," said Robin.
"How about you, Ben?"

"I really want to see a raccoon,"
said Ben, "but I think they only
come out at night."

"Sarah, you'd better watch out
for a big, fat snake," teased
a boy, his brown eyes
wide with mischief.

"I'm not afraid, Thomas!" answered Sarah.
"Come on, let's go! I want to see the otters.
They're the best! They swim so fast and
have the cutest faces."

Mr. Gator couldn't believe his ears. He might not have the cutest face, but surely he was the best animal in the lake. He certainly was the biggest and the bravest.

"What about me?" Mr. Gator wanted to shout. "Doesn't anyone want to see me?" But the children, never seeing the alligator, walked on down the path, leaving poor Mr. Gator all alone.

Mr. Gator didn't know what to do. He thought
everyone came to the lake to see him. Well, if no one
wanted to see him anymore, he didn't have to stay!
He decided to look for a new home where
he could be more appreciated.

"I have it!" he thought. "I'll cross over the dam into the creek. Surely, someone there will notice my fine alligator qualities." He climbed up the bank by the rose vines, and quickly slid down the other side, disturbing a kingfisher from its favorite perch.

Since the tide was low, he was careful to avoid the sharp, crusty oyster beds that bordered the salt marsh.

Making his way through the dark, squishy pluff mud,
Mr. Gator finally reached the creek and swam up a narrow
channel toward deeper water. Cordgrass and salt air
welcomed him to his new surroundings.

Looking ahead, he saw two dolphins gracefully leaping out of the creek. "They must be coming to greet me," thought Mr. Gator, putting on his friendliest smile. But as he swam closer, the dolphins quickly disappeared under the water.

Mr. Gator was hungry! He realized he had missed his breakfast, so he decided to go fishing. Soon he saw a spot-tailed bass swimming his way.

Mr. Gator opened his powerful jaws for the catch, but before he could enjoy his meal, a brown pelican swooped down and gulped the fish up into its huge beak.

"This is my fishing territory, you overgrown lizard," squawked the pelican. "Go away!"

Mr. Gator was so startled by the pelican that he dove down, down under the water to escape, almost bumping into a fierce-looking garfish armed with scary sharp teeth.

Reaching the bottom of the creek, he saw a flat flounder
trying to disguise itself in the sand, and blue crabs scurrying
sideways out of harm's way.

Being a curious alligator, he swam closer for a better look.
CRUNCH! A large blue crab's razor-sharp claw latched on to
Mr. Gator's snout.

"YOW!" screamed Mr. Gator, shooting straight up and out of the
water. The crab held on to Mr. Gator's snout with all of its might.

"Take that, you rude, ravenous reptile!" snarled the crab in its
crabbiest voice. "Maybe next time you'll watch where you stick
your long, snoopy snout."

Flying over to check out the fuss, laughing gulls giggled at the silly sight.

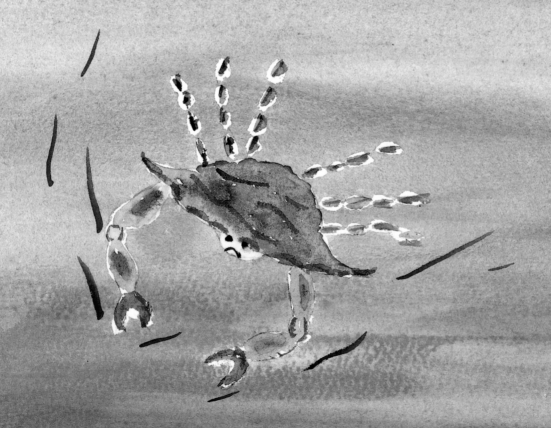

Exhausted from its speech, the crab let go and fell with a splish
and a plunk back into the creek.

Mr. Gator's snout throbbed with pain as he moped along, feeling
sorry for himself. This wasn't the way it was supposed to be.
Maybe his old lake home wasn't so bad after all, even if the children
didn't want to see him anymore.

Suddenly, he heard a roaring sound coming from behind, growing louder—and louder—and louder!

Turning to look, Mr. Gator saw a speeding motorboat racing toward him. Just in time, he swerved out of the way. The boat sped past with its roaring motor churning the water like rapids on a wild river.

"That does it!" said Mr. Gator. "I'm going home— this is no place for me!"

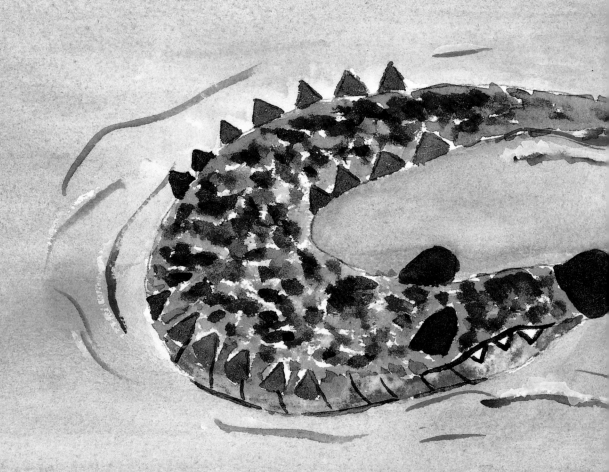

The tide had come in, making it easier to swim back through the channel that led to safety. Reaching the creek bank, he crawled back up and over the dam to the comforts of home.

Mr. Gator swam toward a sunny bank for a late afternoon nap. On the way, he spotted the same children he had seen earlier that morning.

"Oh no," he sighed sadly. "I know they don't want to see me."

But before he could swim away, he heard one of them shout, "There he is, the alligator! Isn't he amazing?"

"He's more than amazing," said Ben. "He's awesome! He's the one we've all been waiting to see."

"Yeah!" said Thomas, with a nod and a grin. "There are a lot of great animals to see on the lake ... but that old alligator is the best animal of all."

Mr. Gator's Glossary

Bank: an elevation of rising ground alonga lake, creek, river, etc.

Cordgrass (SPARTINA): the most abundant salt marsh plant in South Carolina, responsible for much of the marsh's productivity.

Creek: a body of water smaller than a river but larger than a brook. Saltwater creeks rise and fall with the tide.

Dam: a barrier that stops the flow of water.

Garfish: a fierce, hungry fish with slender jaws, long bill, and sharp teeth. Garfish vary in size from 2 feet to 5 feet.

Kingfisher: a blue-gray, pigeon-sized bird with a bushy crest and a dagger-like bill. Kingfishers live and fish along rivers, lakes, and saltwater marshes.

Laughing Gull: a medium-sized gull with a black hood in summer. It lacks a hood in winter. These birds make a loud, high-pitched "ha ha ha ha haah" call. They easily catch food that is tossed in the air.

Pelican: a large, fish-eating, web-footed bird with an expanding pouch under the lower jaw, which it uses to capture and store fish.

Salt Marsh: a wet area where non-woody plants such as cordgrass, needlerush, sedges, and rushes grow. Saltwater marshes lie along coasts between land and water. They are affected by tides twice a day.